SPOTLIGHT ON NATIVE AMERICANS

CREE

Trevor Grailey

New York

Published in 2016 by The Rosen Publishing Group, Inc.
29 East 21st Street, New York, NY 10010

First Edition

Editor: Karolena Bielecki
Book Design: Kris Everson
Reviewed by: Robert J. Conley, Former Sequoyah Distinguished Professor at Western Carolina University and Director of Native American Studies at Morningside College and Montana State University
Supplemental material reviewed by: Donald A. Grinde, Jr., Professor of Transnational/American Studies at the State University of New York at Buffalo.

Photo Credits: Cover Mychele Daniau/AFP/Getty Images; pp. 4–5 © Mark Coffey/All Canada Photos/age fotostock; pp. 7, 8, 15 North Wind Picture Archives; p. 11 Peter Newark's American Pictures; pp. 13, 20, 29 Corbis; p. 19 © Interfoto/age fotostock; pp. 22–23 Nativestock.com/Marilyn Angel Wynn/The Image Bank/Getty Images; p. 25 © Tim Graham/Robert Harding Picture Library/age fotostock; pp. 26–27 BGSmith/Shutterstock.com.

Library of Congress Cataloging-in-Publication Data

Grailey, Trevor.
 Cree / Trevor Grailey.
     pages cm. — (Spotlight on Native Americans)
 Includes bibliographical references and index.
 ISBN 978-1-4994-1707-4 (pbk.)
 ISBN 978-1-4994-1705-0 (6 pack)
 ISBN 978-1-4994-1709-8 (library binding)
1. Cree Indians—History—Juvenile literature. 2. Cree Indians—Social life and customs—Juvenile literature. I. Title.
 E99.C88G73 2016
 971.2004'97323—dc23
                                        2015009260

Manufactured in the United States of America

CONTENTS

CREE LAND AND ORIGIN

CHAPTER 1

The Cree **Nation** once roamed a huge area in Canada east of the Hudson and the James Bays, as far west as Alberta and as far south as Lake Superior. Today, it is the largest Native American nation in Canada (where Indian tribes are called First Nations). Over 200,000 Crees live in Canada, and many live in the United States, too.

Crees tell a traditional origin story. In the beginning, the Crees lived in the land above. A man and a woman decided to go to the land below. As a spider lowered them on a line, it warned them not to look down until they reached the ground. They looked, so the line stopped, leaving them stuck atop a tall tree.

They asked many animals to carry them down, but only the bear and wolverine would help. The couple followed the bear, which taught them survival. According to this origin story, all the Crees are descended from these two people.

The Cree tribe was divided into two major **cultures**. The culture of the Western Woods Crees (or Woodland Crees) was based upon hunting and trapping in the forests of the cold north. Buffalo hunting formed the basis of the culture of the Plains Crees.

The Plains Crees moved to the plains of Saskatchewan to hunt the buffalo that roamed there.

WESTERN WOODS CREE HISTORY

CHAPTER 2

The Western Woods Crees included many different Cree bands, or groups. For hundreds of years, they lived off the land by hunting and trapping animals or fishing. All these bands spoke a similar language. Demand for furs in Europe brought French traders to Cree country, where they set up trading posts. Excellent hunters and trappers, the Crees exchanged beaver pelts for trade goods, such as guns and household items, first with the French and then with the British.

Trading posts also hired many Crees as hunters to supply them with meat. For a short time, the Crees were a rich, powerful tribe. As the supply of animals dwindled, however, the Crees had to keep moving south and west to look for more game. They were so busy hunting and trapping for the traders that many were no longer **self-sufficient** and couldn't live entirely off the land. By 1717, many Western Woods Crees depended upon the Hudson's Bay Company for guns, cloth, blankets, and some of their food. This changed their traditional lifestyle.

During the 1800s, fur dealers arrived by wagon and boat at the Hudson's Bay Company's trading posts to buy and sell furs bound for Europe.

When Europeans arrived in North America, they brought diseases that killed more Native Americans than all other causes combined, including war. In 1781, a smallpox **epidemic** wiped out about half of the Cree population.

CHANGES FOR THE WESTERN WOODS CREES

CHAPTER 3

Semipermanent native communities sprang up around trading posts, with religious **missions** located nearby. The missionaries tried to **convert** the Western Woods

Missionaries preached to the fur traders and Native Americans. Many had little respect for the traditional native spiritual practices they were trying to replace.

Crees to Christianity. Many Crees also abandoned their traditional handmade goods for Canadian supplies.

Throughout the nineteenth century, few Europeans settled in the cold north. Then, lumber companies disturbed the heavily forested lands. In treaties signed between 1876 and 1906, the Western Woods Crees traded most of their traditional lands to the Canadian government in exchange for **reserves** and promised social services.

From 1920 to 1940, many diseases that were new to the Crees, such as measles and influenza, hit them hard. After World War II (1939–1945), government services, such as schools and health clinics, turned old trading posts into villages. The Crees lived here year-round, though the men left on hunting trips during the winter.

By the 1940s, the Crees depended upon the Canadian government for their living. The market for fur was gone, and fewer Western Woods Crees lived in traditional ways. Beginning in the late 1940s until the 1970s, most Cree children were sent away to boarding schools where they learned English. They forgot how to speak Cree and learned no traditional skills.

PLAINS CREE HISTORY

CHAPTER 4

The scarcity of winter game had forced the Plains Cree to move onto the Great Plains in southern Saskatchewan and Alberta to hunt buffalo, thus emerging as a distinct group. They also became agents for European traders, exchanging goods with other tribes for furs to bring to the trading posts.

Allied with the Blackfoot Indians, the Crees began to live like other Great Plains natives. Buffalo skins provided clothing and shelter, while buffalo meat fed the people.

Between 1810 and 1850, the Plains Crees moved farther into the Great Plains areas but had problems getting enough horses. Known as the "Horse Wars," the Crees stole or fought to capture horses from other tribes.

Between 1850 and 1880, buffalo began to vanish from the Great Plains, killed by Americans for their hides. The Crees entered other tribes' territories in the United States to hunt buffalo, which led to warfare. Members of the Blackfoot tribe drove the Crees out of

Rindisbacher. This 1826 painting by Peter Rindisbacher shows a Plains Cree man chasing a buffalo with his dogs. Crees often hunted buffalo by frightening the animals so they ran into pens or a marsh, trapping them and making them easy targets.

their territory in today's southern Canada and northern Montana, defeating their former allies at the Battle of Old Man River in 1871.

The starving Plains Crees requested a treaty with the Canadian government. In exchange for Cree lands, the treaty promised them farming tools, seeds, a yearly payment, and schools.

PLAINS CREE ALLIANCE WITH MÉTIS

CHAPTER 5

In 1885, Canadian Louis Riel led the Métis (who were the **descendants** of Native Americans and Europeans, usually people from France) in an uprising against the Canadian government because it refused to admit the Métis had any claims to their lands. Plains Cree chiefs Poundmaker and Big Bear sided with the Métis. Some members of Big Bear's band killed settlers at Frog Lake on the Alberta–Saskatchewan border. Eight Cree warriors were convicted of murder. Both Big Bear and Poundmaker were convicted of treason and sentenced to three years in prison. Big Bear's son led the rest of his band across the border to Montana, where they joined an Ojibwe band. Their descendants continue to live there today.

By the late 1800s, Christian missionaries had converted many Plains Crees to Christianity and worked to end traditional religious practices. From 1884 to 1921, for example, the Sun Dance, an important Cree ritual, was outlawed in Canada. Many traditional ceremonies were held in secret. World War II (1939–1945) saw more and

Louis Riel spent his life fighting for the rights of the Métis.

better social services for the Plains Crees. Plains Cree children went to missionary schools, while their parents, who were no longer able to live off the land, looked for paying jobs and government allowances to help them survive.

WESTERN WOODS CREE TRADITIONAL LIFE

CHAPTER 6

Western Woods Cree children were named several months after birth. The baby was often kept on a cradleboard with moss diapers. As children grew older, they had to help their parents.

Western Woods Cree teenagers fasted alone for a short time to gain powers from the spirits that appeared in their dreams or visions. When a boy killed his first big-game animal—at about 14 years old—a feast was held in his honor. A girl reaching **puberty** stayed in a small lodge away from camp for four nights with a wise old woman to tell her stories. She returned to camp to attend a feast.

The Western Woods Crees traveled on snowshoes and toboggans during the long winter, as well as by canoes and dog **travois** in the summer. When everything froze, activity slowed, except when the men went hunting and trapping. In spring, the Crees sprang into action for great caribou hunts. As soon as the rivers thawed, Cree bands paddled canoes to their summer camp, gathering

At first, Cree babies were carried in a hide sack stuffed with moss. The introduction of the cradleboard gave the Crees another way to carry their babies.

at a lakeshore for fishing, berry picking, and visiting. By autumn, the bands would leave by canoe and scatter to their winter hunting grounds.

PLAINS CREE TRADITIONAL LIFE

CHAPTER 7

Soon after the birth of a Plains Cree baby, a medicine man or woman would name him or her—based on a vision or dream—at a feast.

A key religious ceremony, the Sun Dance was also a social event for the Cree people that featured dancing, gambling, and courting.

Older children spent most of their time with their grandparents, who told them stories and taught them skills. Teenage boys taught the younger ones how to hunt and fight. When girls went through puberty, they went on a vision quest. Teenage boys also went on a vision quest. During a boy's dream or vision, an animal spirit helper would appear, describe the gifts being given to the young man (such as the ability to lead war parties or cure the sick), and teach him a power song.

The most important Plains Cree ceremony was the Sun Dance, which was given to honor the thunder or the sun. The participants did not eat or drink during the four-day ceremony but sang and danced throughout. During the Smoking Spirit ceremony, which was another important event, an all-night singing session honored all the spirits. Buffalo dances were held to assure good hunting. The Crees smoked a pipe as an offering to the supernatural and used sweat baths and the smoke from burning sweetgrass to clean and purify themselves.

CREE LEADERSHIP AND BELIEFS

CHAPTER 8

The Western Woods Crees were organized into bands made up of family members; they had no formal government. Leaders were men chosen for their hunting ability, experience, and spiritual power.

The Crees have kept many of their traditional religious beliefs private. The Crees believed that sickness and injuries were the results of evil spirits at work. Helping spirits, or manitous, came to them in dreams or visions and gave them special powers or protection for hunting or warfare. Animals had spirits, too.

The Crees believed that during the hunt, the hunter made a connection with the animal being hunted, and the animal decided whether or not to give itself to the hunter.

The Plains Crees were organized in groups of small bands, some of which had more than one chief. Councils of leading men made decisions for the band. Basing their decision on the chief's hunting ability, wealth, and generosity, people chose the band they wanted to join. Each band had a warrior society, to which most of the younger men belonged. The warrior society gave food to needy people and organized the large buffalo hunts.

Shown here is a nineteenth-century color engraving of Cree chief Mähsette-Kuiuab.

WORKING TOGETHER
CHAPTER 9

During the last half of the twentieth century, European Canadians spread into traditional Cree hunting grounds and homelands, disturbing the traditional way of life for the Crees. Instead of roaming the forests, Crees settled permanently onto numerous scattered reserves in Canada and even one

This photograph shows a meeting to discuss Cree land issues on November 19, 1974.

reservation in the United States, as well as in many different Canadian cities and towns. They began to rely upon the Canadian government to provide education, housing, food, and medical care.

Realizing that the Canadian government had not followed through on its treaty promises, Crees became politically active in the 1960s. Plains Cree John Tootoosis founded and led the Federation of Saskatchewan Indians in 1958 and was active in the National Indian Brotherhood. These and other **activist** groups worked hard to ensure that the Canadian government fulfilled all the rights listed in the treaties signed in exchange for Cree land.

The Crees of northern Quebec are represented by the Grand Council of the Crees. This council was set up in 1974. Today, it works to promote the interests of the local Crees, such as preserving traditional lifestyles and improving conditions in Cree communities.

CREES IN THE UNITED STATES TODAY

CHAPTER 10

A group of Plains Crees fled to Montana in the 1880s and joined with an Ojibwe (Chippewa) band. In 1916, they were given the Rocky Boy Indian Reservation in northern Montana, which is only 40 miles (64 km) from the Canadian border. In 1935, they were recognized by the United States government as the Chippewa Cree Tribe.

Today, the tribe has more than 5,000 members, with about 3,300 living on the reservation. The largest of the

Chippewa Cree communities is Box Elder, with around 750 people. It is also one of the poorest, with more than half of the population living below the poverty line. In 2007, the tribe opened a casino, which provides jobs and income for the tribe. The Chippewa Cree Tribe celebrates traditional culture at gatherings, including an annual **powwow** in August.

Special Head Start Programs teach Cree children traditional singing, drumming, storytelling, and language in preschool. Many elementary schools teach kindergarten through third grades only in Cree, and some children now speak the language better than their parents. Cree groups sponsor older children in Cree culture camps during the summer, where they learn the "bush skills" needed to live off the land.

Chippewa Cree men in traditional dress are shown here dancing during the annual powwow on the Rocky Boy Indian Reservation in Montana.

CONTEMPORARY ARTS

CHAPTER 11

Cree people participate in modern arts as well as traditional styles. Along with paintings and sculptures, Cree artists create moccasins, complex beadwork, and birch-bark boxes.

Albertan author and artist George Littlechild illustrates children's picture books that he and others have written. One example is *This Land Is My Land*, which is a book that describes his experience growing up as a Cree boy in Canada.

Jane Ash Poitras is a famous Cree artist from Alberta whose paintings hang in U.S. and Canadian museums. One of her works is a large exhibit that took three years to create. Called *Who Discovered the Americas?*, this mixture of preexisting images and paintings shows the effects of Christopher Columbus's "discovery" on Native Americans. Poitras's recent work also features the themes of native medicine and healing plants.

Allen Sapp was born on a reserve in Saskatchewan in 1928. His paintings portray scenes of Cree life from his early years. Sapp was honored as an Officer of the Order

First Nations people, such as the Crees, are renowned for their complex beadwork.

of Canada in 1986. His illustrations for the children's book *The Song Within My Heart* (2003) won the Governor General's Award.

CREE ISSUES
CHAPTER 12

During the 1990s, the Canadian First Nations (including the Crees) and the Canadian government worked together to review the original treaties and settle any remaining treaty issues. This has resulted in many Cree bands signing a "Treaty Land Entitlement Agreement" and gaining additional lands in order to fulfill the original treaty agreement.

More than 100 years after Poundmaker was convicted of treason for his part in the 1885 rebellion, a Canadian television show has questioned Poundmaker's conviction. The show used the original trial **transcripts** to re-create Poundmaker's trial on film. The filmmakers say that the historical records show that Poundmaker was innocent, and they have asked the Canadian justice department to review his case.

Modern Crees face a number of health issues and ecological concerns. For example, the Mikisew Crees of Fort Chipewyan depend on the Athabasca River. It provides them with drinking water and fish, but it is highly polluted as a result of crude oil production. The Crees have noticed that many of the fish are now deformed. They have also realized that more people are getting ill, and some are now sick with a rare cancer. The Mikisew Crees believe the oil industry is to blame.

Athabasca River, Alberta, Canada

REBUILDING A COMMUNITY

CHAPTER 13

The Oujé-Bougoumou Crees live in northern Quebec. In the 1940s, outsiders set up mining operations on their land, which is a process that has increased ever since. The tribe has seen its villages destroyed and was relocated seven times until 1970.

After many years of fighting for their rights, the Crees received money from the Quebec government to build a new, permanent village on the shores of Lake Opemisca. They chose the famous native architect Douglas Cardinal to design the village. The new buildings were influenced by traditional Cree structures. The houses have open beams, skylights, and doors that face east. The village's heating system uses waste sawdust from a local sawmill as a fuel in a central boiler house.

The Aanischaaukamikw Cultural Institute was built in Oujé-Bougoumou in 2011. Its visible beams and curved shape mimic the traditional Cree gathering space where feasts were held.

Anna and David Bosum set up a business offering cultural tours based around Oujé-Bougoumou. Visitors experience traditional Cree life while taking part in summer canoe trips.

The Crees continue to fight to maintain their traditional culture and teach their children the Cree language and the importance of living off the land. As their prosperity and education increase, the Crees have more choices, and they are choosing to embrace their traditional culture and values whenever they can.

GLOSSARY

activist: A person who acts strongly in support of or against an issue.

allied: Joined in a relationship in which people or groups agree to work together.

convert: To bring over from one belief or view to another.

culture: The arts, beliefs, and customs that form a people's way of life.

descendant: Proceeding from people who lived long before you.

epidemic: An outbreak of a disease that spreads quickly and affects many people at one time.

mission: A church or group of buildings where people of one religion try to teach people of another religion their beliefs.

nation: People who have their own customs, laws, and land separate from other nations or people.

powwow: A Native America social gathering.

puberty: The period during which a person becomes capable of reproducing.

reservation: Land set aside by the U.S. government for specific Native American tribes to live on.

reserve: Land set aside by the Canadian government for specific Native American tribes to live on.

self-sufficient: Able to live or function without help or support from others.

transcript: An official or legal printed copy of something.

travois: A simple vehicle consisting of two poles joined by a frame and typically pulled by an animal.

FOR MORE INFORMATION

BOOKS

Bial, Raymond. *The Cree.* New York, NY: Marshall
   Cavendish, 2005.
Robinson, Deborah B. *The Cree of North America.*
   Minneapolis, MN: Lerner Publications Co., 2002.
Ryan, Marla Felkins, and Linda Schmittroth. *Cree.*
   San Diego, CA: Blackbirch Press, 2003.

WEBSITES

Due to the changing nature of Internet links, PowerKids Press has developed an online list of websites related to the subject of this book. This site is updated regularly. Please use this link to access the list: www.powerkidslinks.com/sona/cree

INDEX

A
Alberta, 4, 10, 12, 24, 27
art, 24, 25
Athabasca River, 27

B
Big Bear, 12
Blackfoot, 10
books, 24, 25
buffalo, 5, 10, 11, 18

C
Canadian government, 9, 11, 12,
        21, 26

F
Federation of Saskatchewan
        Indians, 21

G
Grand Council of the Crees, 21
Great Plains, 10

H
Hudson's Bay Company, 6, 7

M
Métis, 12, 13
Montana, 11, 12, 22, 23

N
National Indian Brotherhood, 21

O
Ojibwe, 12, 22

P
Poundmaker, 12, 26, 27

Q
Quebec, 21, 28

R
Riel, Louis, 12, 13

S
Saskatchewan, 5, 10, 12, 24
smallpox, 7
Sun Dance, 12, 16, 17

U
United States government, 22

V
visions, 14, 16, 17, 18